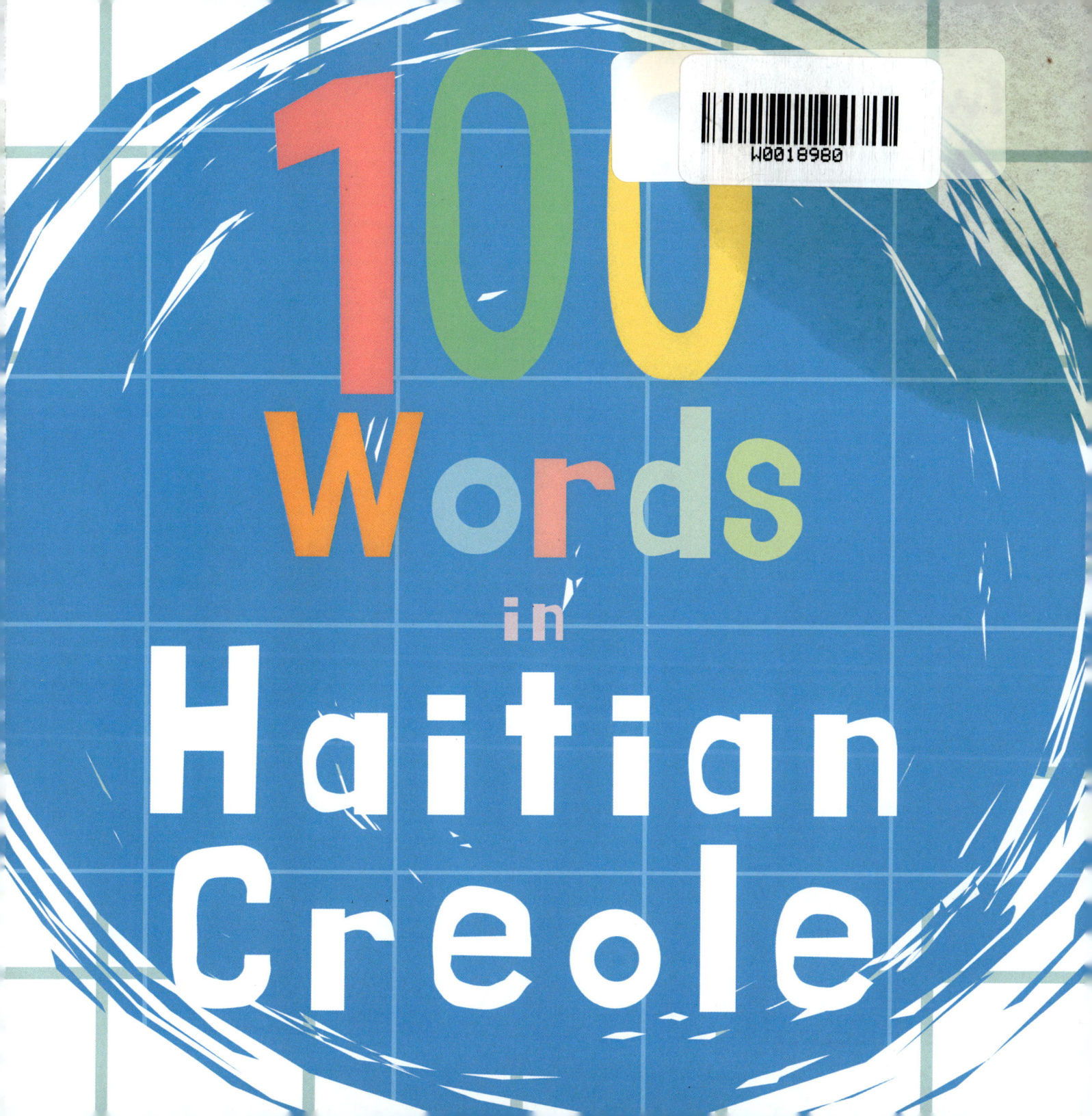

100 Words in Haitian Creole

fwi · fruits

bannann
bananas

seriz
cherries

fwaz
strawberry

mango
mango

melon dlo
watermelon

legim · vegetables

tomat
tomato

zonyon
onion

kawòt
carrot

pòmdetè
potatoes

pwav
pepper

bèt · animals

tòti
turtle

chwal
horse

krapo
frog

chen
dog

lou
wolf

ti chen
puppy

kizin · kitchen

boukliye
kettle

chodyè
pot

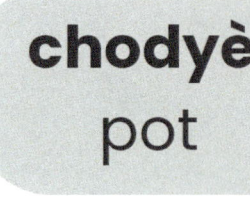

plak
plate

kwit manje
cook

kiyè
spoon

frijidè
fridge

kouto
knife

fouchèt
fork

manje · food

ze
egg

pen
bread

bè
butter

vyann
meat

poul
chicken

yogout
yogurt

kay · house

twalèt
bathroom

salon
living room

fenèt
window

eskalye
stairs

pòt
door

twa
roof

chanm · room

chèz
chair

tapi
carpet

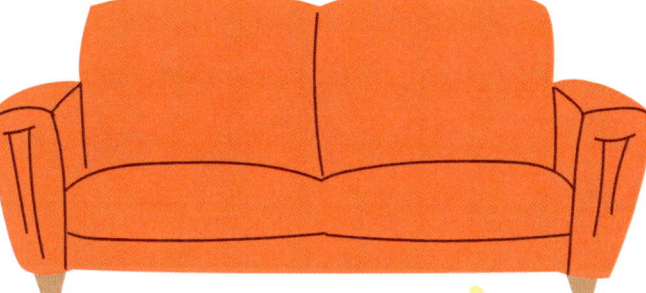

pòtre
poster

sofa
sofa

tab
table

lanp
lamp

koule · colors

jòn
yellow

ble
blue

vèt
green

blan
white

nwa
black

wouj
red

woz
pink

fòm · shapes

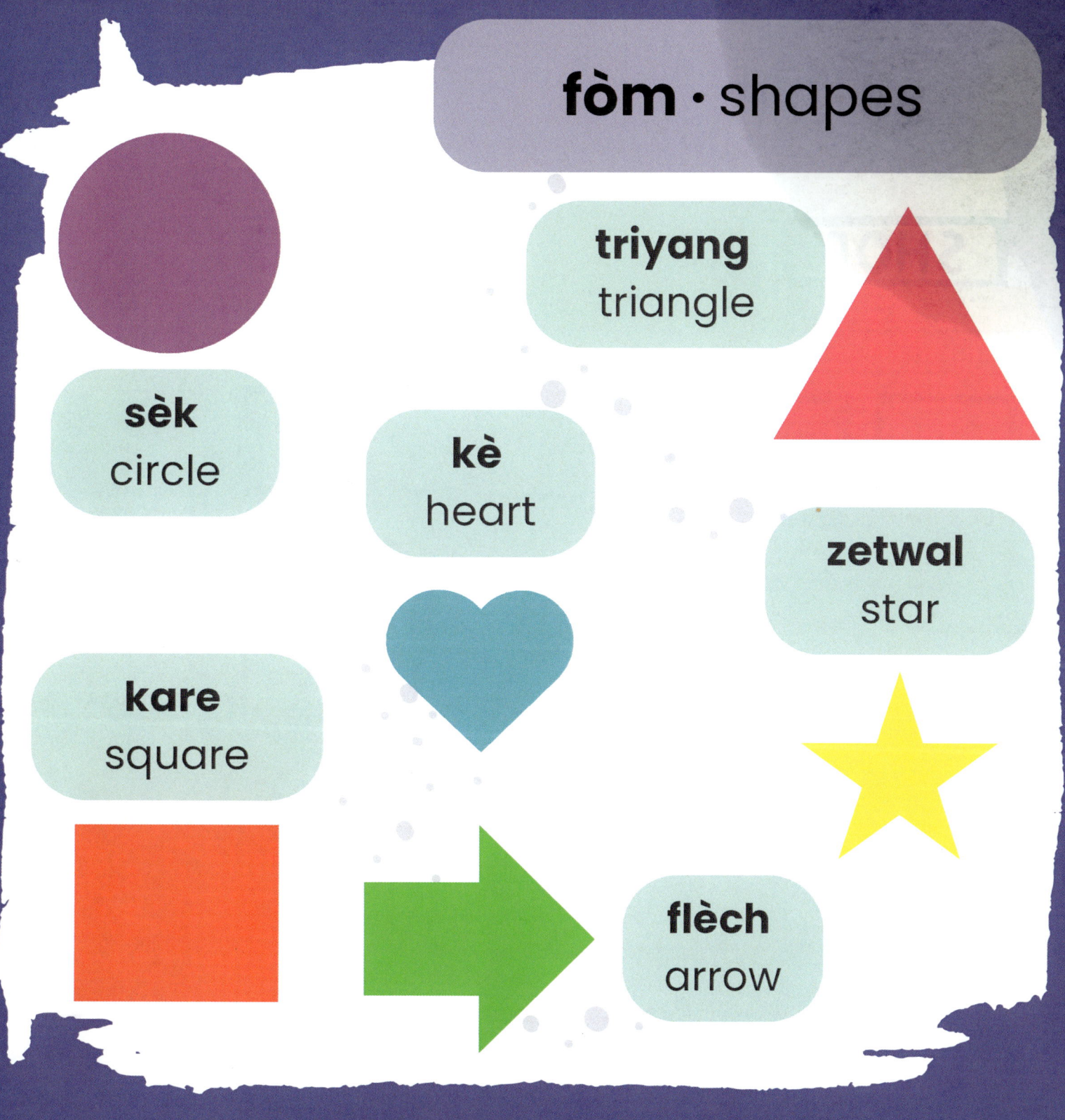

triyang
triangle

sèk
circle

kè
heart

zetwal
star

kare
square

flèch
arrow

vil · city

magazen
shop

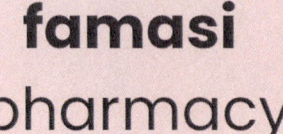

famasi
pharmacy

lopital
hospital

boulanje
bakery

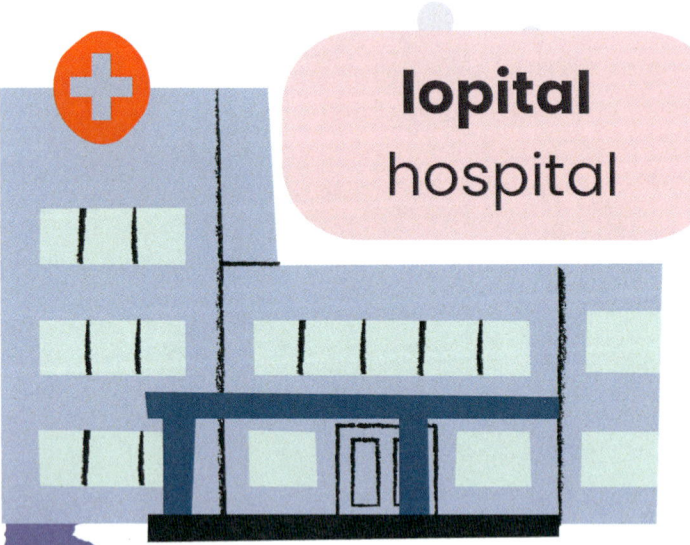

machin · vehicles

machin
car

kamyon
truck

fouye
digger

bis
bus

anbilans
ambulance

nimewo · numbers

youn
one

de
two

twa
three

kat
four

senk
five

6 sis
six

sèt
seven

7

8 uit
eight

9 nèf
nine

10 dis
ten

ete · summer

krèm glas
ice cream

chapo
hat

solèy
sun

pèl
shovel

chato sab
sand castle

bokit
bucket

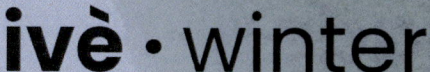

ivè · winter

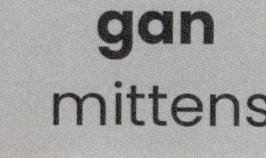

gan
mittens

nèj
snow

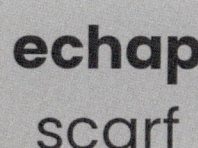

echap
scarf

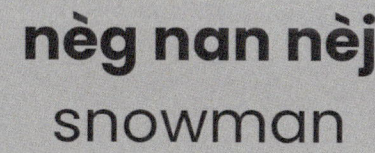

nèg nan nèj
snowman

Papa Nwèl
Santa Claus

jaden · garden

po flè
flowerpot

papiyon
butterfly

flè
flowers

dlo pou wouze
watering can

bibit
ladybug

nwa
clouds

nechèl
ladder

jadenye
gardener

pye bwa
tree

zèb
grass

fanmi · family

pitit gason
son

pitit fi
daughter

manman
mother

papa
father

frè
brother

sè
sister

granpapa
grandfather

grann
grandmother

pitit pitit gason
grandson

pitit pitit fi
granddaughter

rad · clothes

mayo
t-shirt

pantalon
trousers

soulye
shoes

sak
handbag

chosèt
socks

bout
pantalon
shorts

rob
dress

pantouf
slippers

YOU ALREADY KNOW OVER 100 WORDS IN HAITIAN CREOLE!

Made in United States
Orlando, FL
02 March 2026

100 words

English
Haitian Creole

Discovering a bilingual world has to start somewhere. In this book, your little one will find basic words that will make learning a new language easier!

ISBN 9798345415122